Pierrot

DAVID BUSSELL
But... You're a Horse

But... You're a Horse

David Bussell is an award-winning British humourist whose work has featured in *The Huffington Post, Buzzfeed, B3TA, Digital Spy,* and (quite without his permission) *The Daily Mail.*

Born in 1976, David grew increasingly larger until he reached adulthood. Among his interests are amateur parkour, the Oxford comma, and writing about himself in the third person. Rumours that David was conceived on an Indian burial ground remain largely unfounded. David would beat you in a fight.

Things people have said about David Bussell:

"Hilarious" Graham Linehan (*Father Ted, The IT Crowd*)

"Really good" Shane Allen
(*BBC Controller of Comedy Commissioning*)

"Ha!" Sam Bain (*Peep Show, Fresh Meat*)

You can see more from the author by following him on Twitter @Busselling

Copyright © 2014 by David Bussell

All rights reserved. This book or any portion thereof may not be reproduced or used in any manner whatsoever without the express written permission of the author except for the use of brief quotations in a book review.

First Printing, 2014
Second Edition, 2014

ISBN: 978-1-291-74275-6

Introduction

Hello.

Dedication

For Adriana,

While you're out can you swing by Tesco and pick up some 70% dark Lindt chocolate and a packet of Dr Karg's crackers? Thanks, love.

For Publisher,

I meant to write my wife a dedication but accidentally wrote her a shopping list instead. It's not too late to make changes, is it?

For David,

Unfortunately it's not possible to make amendments at this juncture. I don't anticipate this being a problem though, given that no one actually reads dedications.

"Talent borrows, genius steals" ~ David Bussell.

Contents

The cover again, this time in black and white............1
A blurb that the conceited swine obviously wrote himself............2
Copyright guff and a sweary bird............3
Introduction............4
Dedication (oooh ooh, that's what you need)............5
A blank page............6
Thought-provoking quote............7
Contents............8
Yet more contents............9
Knock Knock hijack: Part one............10
Looks like I win this round, Hitler............14
Suicide Squirrels............16
Conan the Rejected: Part one............20
Out of Office............21
Do you have any copies of A1?............22
Don't take my wife... please!............27
Mad Men 1980s: Guess Who............28
First draft chat-up lines............31
Terror flight!............32
A.C.E.d it............33
Solipsistic wrestlers............34
Top picks for the Fringe Festival............35
All-purpose phrases I find useful when I have absolutely no idea what I'm talking about............39
Cats for the blind............40
Knock Knock hijack: Part two............43
Conan the Rejected: Part two............44
Action movie crossovers for the equal opportunities era............45
Selling a haunted house............46
Sample reviews from Potpourri Monthly............54
He is risen!............55
Top Wasp............56

Yet more contents

Photoshop tools I wish I could use on my memories of being a teenager............59
Mad Men 1980s: Rubik's Cube............60
Oxymoron............62
Megaphone City............64
Tragic Google searches............67
Bussfeed............68
Twerk to the Future............69
A Bloke's guide to lip balm............70
Halloween costume ideas............72
XXX Sorority Girls Gone Wild............76
Manly things I have yet to do............84
There can be only mum............85
Conan the Rejected: Part three............86
Four walls and a fuck swing............87
Erotic minutes............88
R.I.P. Mrs Wayne............92
British sitcoms that sound like slang for defecation............93
Deep comedy............94
Awesome pranks, AKA dick moves............99
Animal Porn Boss Screens............100
Conan the Rejected: Part four............101
Mad Men 1980s: Garbage Pail Kids............102
Pride Gardening............105
Baby on board............106
Top ten numbers............108
Conan the Rejected: Part five............109
Knock Knock hijack: Part three............110
Apologies............112
A word from our sponsor............113
Credits............114
Actual credits to prove I am not a monster............115
A gift to God............116

Knock Knock hijack: Part one

I just can't help myself around Steve. The man is a walking Kick Me sign, and I will turn my knee-bone into powder before I tire of putting the boot in. Don't blame me, he brings it upon himself. See, despite mountains of evidence to the contrary, Steve is under the impression that he's a funny man. All I can say to that is, if there's a funny man in Steve, I only hope he's gentle.

Monday mornings are when Steve chooses to light up our lives with the glorious gift of laughter. Which is to say he goes to Facebook and does a cut and paste on some geriatric email forward. His school of thought has it that he's bringing a little sunshine to the start of our working week. Sadly, Steve's school of thought demands an urgent Ofsted report.

My friend Tim and I have come to make the best of a bad situation by hijacking Steve's Knock Knock jokes and giving them the old 9/11. Part of the fun is stepping on his punch line, but the real juice is working Steve into such a frenzy that one day, God willing, he'll dash his brains out with that stupid Blackberry of his.

Steve
whose ready for a monday morning joke guyz?
24 minutes ago via Facebook for Blackberry · Comment · Like

👍 7 people like this

> **Steve** knock knock...
> 23 minutes ago · Like

> **Steve** whose there?
> 23 minutes ago · Like

> **Steve** Irish Stu...
> 23 minutes ago · Like · 👍 1

> **David** Oh hi, Stu, come on in, it's been a while. What brings you round this way?
> 23 minutes ago · Like · 👍 4

> **David** Just passing by, huh? Cool, cool. Just as long as Sarah didn't kick you out of the house, ha ha!
> 22 minutes ago · Like

> **David** *Stu starts crying uncontrollably*
> 22 minutes ago · Like

> **David** Oh shit, she did? Man, I am so sorry, I was just kidding. What the hell happened?
> 22 minutes ago · Like · 👍 1

> **Steve** Can we not do this again Dave I'm just trying to tell a joke
> 20 minutes ago · Like

> **Tim** Knock Knock
> 20 minutes ago · Like · 👍 4

> **David** Wait a second, Stu, I think I hear someone at the door. I'll go get rid of them, I'm sure it's just a salesman...
> 19 minutes ago · Like

> **David** Hello, can I help you?
> 19 minutes ago · Like

> **Tim** I'm batman
> 19 minutes ago · Like · 👍 10

> **Steve** Tim dont encourage him!!
> 18 minutes ago · Like

> **David** Holy heck, it's the caped crusader! What are you doing here?
> 18 minutes ago · Like

Tim I'm not the caped crusader, I'm batman with a little 'b'. I'm here to get rid of your bats.
17 minutes ago · Like · 👍 2

David Oh, I see. Still, it seems weird you'd show up in a bat costume if you're only in pest control. I mean you don't see regular exterminators fumigate houses dressed like giant wood lice.
17 minutes ago · Like

Steve I swear to god guys
16 minutes ago · Like · 👍 1

Tim Alright, you've got me, I'm not in pest control... I'm here to see Stu.
16 minutes ago · Like

David Stu, do you know this guy?
16 minutes ago · Like

David Stu?
15 minutes ago · Like

Tim Why are you crying, Stu? Did you do it? Did you finally leave her?
15 minutes ago · Like

David Wait a second, are you two...?
15 minutes ago · Like

Tim Yes... we're lovers.
12 minutes ago · Like · 👍 10

Steve Seriously Tim fuck off!!!
12 minutes ago · Like · 👍 11

David Well, that explains why Sarah kicked you out.
12 minutes ago · Like

David Doesn't really explain the Batman costume though...
11 minutes ago · Like

Tim Little 'b', and take it up with head office.
11 minutes ago · Like

Tim Stu I know you're hurting right now but this is what we wanted. With Sarah gone we can finally be together
11 minutes ago · Like

Danny knock knock
11 minutes ago · Like · 👍 2

David For heaven's sake, who is this now?
10 minutes ago · Like

12 BUT... YOU'RE A HORSE

Steve ffs dan please can I get back to my joke??
10 minutes ago · Like

Ariane LOL loving this!!!
10 minutes ago · Like · 👍 5

Danny my name is Detective Inspector Hardbottom and I'm investigating a very serious matter. You see there's been... a murder
10 minutes ago · Like · 👍 7

David Oh my God!
9 minutes ago · Like

Steve FUUUUUCK OFFFFFFFF!
9 minutes ago · Like · 👍 5

David But I don't understand, what do you want with me?
9 minutes ago · Like

Tim I'm batman! (little 'b')
9 minutes ago · Like · 👍 11

Danny I'm not here for you or batman (little 'b') I'm here for your Gaelic friend over there.
8 minutes ago · Like

Steve you don't stop right now i'm unfreinding the lot of u
8 minutes ago · Like

Tim (I'm liking where this is going...)
8 minutes ago · Like

Danny Stuart please put your hands where I can see them, I'm booking you for the bloody murder of your wife, Sarah. In other words... IRISH STU IN THE NAME OF THE LAW
7 minutes ago · Like · 👍 13

Tim POW!
7 minutes ago · Like · 👍 2

David TRIPLE HIGH FIVE FREEZE FRAME!
7 minutes ago · Like · 👍 1

Steve Sriously you can all get fucked
7 minutes ago · Like

Looks like I win this round, Hitler

I remember, back in the eighties, seeing the slogan, 'FREE NELSON MANDELA', daubed onto a brick wall in bright blue paint. It was a powerful, unifying sentiment, spoiled only slightly by the words written in another hand beneath it: '...WITH EVERY BOX OF CORNFLAKES'.

At my local pub, some doomsayer carved the words 'NO FATE' into a table, a la Sarah Connor in Terminator 2. It was only a matter of days before the pub's canny landlord amended it to read 'NO PÂTÉ', a phrase that served both as a Dadaist poem *and* a reflection of the venue's somewhat limited lunch menu.

At another bar, scrawled inside a toilet cubicle, I once found the timeless message 'I FUCKED UR MUM'. Below it someone had written 'GO HOME DAD, YOU'RE DRUNK'. I'm willing to bet the genius who came up with that did a knee slide that put him on the other side of the Channel.

What follows is my humble entry into the hallowed canon of graffiti remedies...

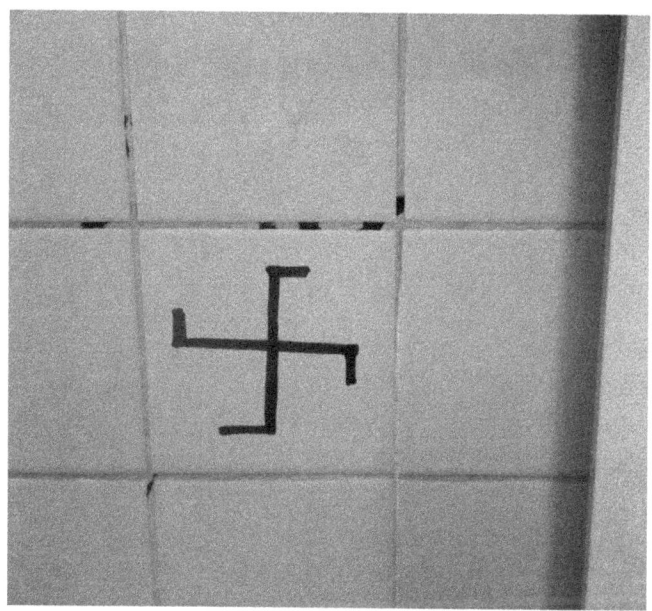

Nazi's, eh? Little beggars. Thankfully, I happened to have a pen with me that day, so I gave the drawing a wee tweak...

Suicide Squirrels

The story goes like this...

My flat has a window box,

My girlfriend and I once saw a squirrel burying a nut in that window box,

My girlfriend and I thought this was adorable,

I was looking for an adorable way to propose to my girlfriend,

So I buried the engagement ring in the window box next to a pile of adorable dirt to kid my girlfriend into thinking the adorable squirrel had returned and done some more adorable burying,

My girlfriend dug into the window box to see what the adorable squirrel had buried this time, and in doing so unearthed the adorable engagement ring,

I swooped in and proposed,

I am adorable,

We are adorable.

And that's how our wedding came to be squirrel-themed. Squirrel invitations, squirrel decorations, even squirrel party favours in the shape of miniature squirrel figurines. My freshly minted fiancé came up with the idea for those, and shopped around to find the best squirrel figurines money could buy. I let her get on with it, and it was only after I saw a hundred or so Sylvanian Family squirrels arrayed on our living room floor that I realised my mistake.

Thanks to my negligence, my guy friends were about come to my wedding only to be sent home with a handful of frilly little girl toys. This was a blow to my machismo that even a heterosexual marriage wouldn't deflect. Something had to be done. I needed to have my say - after all, didn't I have a stake in this marriage too, no matter how small?

I went to my fiancé and shared my concerns (read: gay panic), and after she was done mocking me, she agreed to a compromise. If my masculinity was really so fragile, I had permission to customise the male squirrels to make them a tad more manly. Here's how that went down...

18 BUT... YOU'RE A HORSE

20 BUT... YOU'RE A HORSE

Out of Office

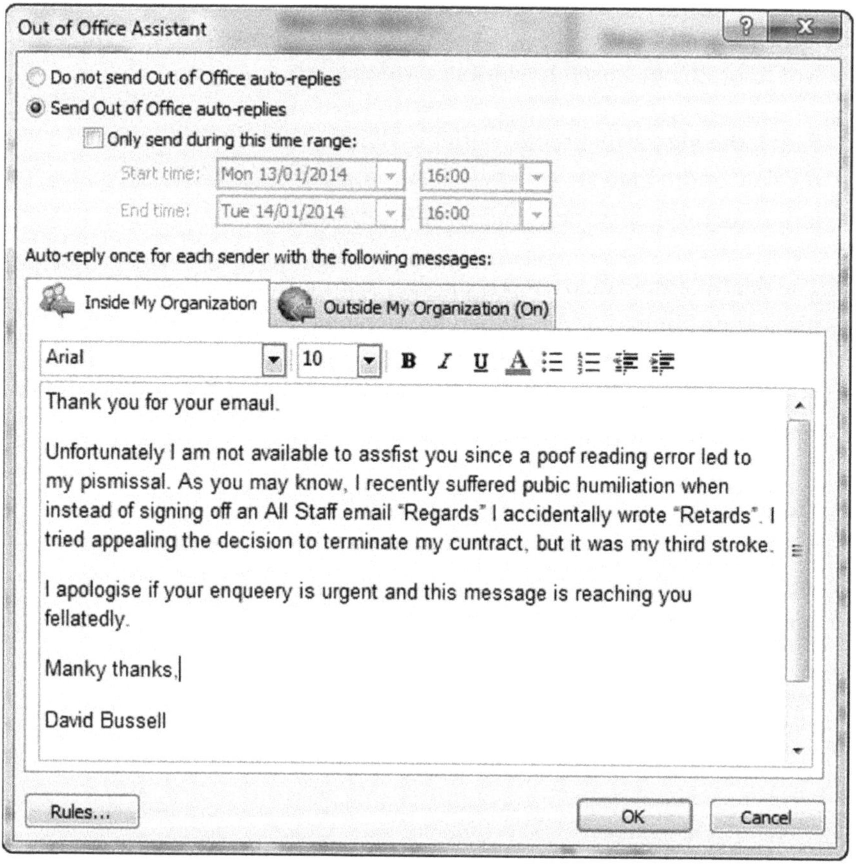

Out of Office Assistant

○ Do not send Out of Office auto-replies
● Send Out of Office auto-replies
  ☐ Only send during this time range:
    Start time: Mon 13/01/2014 16:00
    End time: Tue 14/01/2014 16:00

Auto-reply once for each sender with the following messages:

| Inside My Organization | Outside My Organization (On) |

Arial | 10 | **B** *I* U A

Thank you for your emaul.

Unfortunately I am not available to assfist you since a poof reading error led to my pismissal. As you may know, I recently suffered pubic humiliation when instead of signing off an All Staff email "Regards" I accidentally wrote "Retards". I tried appealing the decision to terminate my cuntract, but it was my third stroke.

I apologise if your enqueery is urgent and this message is reaching you fellatedly.

Manky thanks,

David Bussell

Rules...   OK   Cancel

DAVID BUSSELL 21

Do you have any copies of A1?

Not to brag, but I used to work in a video shop.

Sadly, the high street rental outlet is all but a memory now; gone the way of the high street travel agent, the high street Woolworths and something historians call an "Avril Lavigne".

The death of the video shop is one big tear on the cheek of the discerning cinephile who valued the personal touch (ie being talked down to by a socially marginalised twenty-something who hated you to your very core because you once returned a Bruce Springsteen CD in a Chronicles of Riddick case).

Yes, there are many reasons the video shop floundered - the arrival of mail-order DVDs, online streaming and illegal torrents to name just a few - but it's customer experiences such as the following that really hammered the stake home...

Customer: "Excuse me, do you have any copies of A1?"

Clerk: "You mean late nineties English-Norwegian pop group, A1? I'm afraid you'd want a record shop for that sort of thing."

Customer: "No, I mean the Spielberg film with that boy from the Sixth Sense. You know, A1?"

Clerk: "I don't believe Haley Joel Osment has ever been in a film called A1. He *has* been in a film called A.I. Is it at all possible you're talking about A.I.? Short for Artificial Intelligence?"

Customer: "Yes, that's the one. Please may I have it?"

Clerk: "I'm sorry, but my colleague over there just rented out the last copy while you were busy behaving like a stool-headed gnome-fucker. Good day."

Another contributing factor to the video store's demise was late fees, which amounted to looking a fellow human being in the eye and asserting that because they'd left a copy of the 1994 film Time Cop in their VHS player (RRP £7.99), they now owed £56 and a display of heartfelt contrition.

That said, I'd often take pity on members and warn them when they were starting to rack up serious late fees. The company I worked for provided a template letter to send in such instances, but I found it more satisfying to dispatch custom warnings inspired by the customer's overdue video, hence the following...

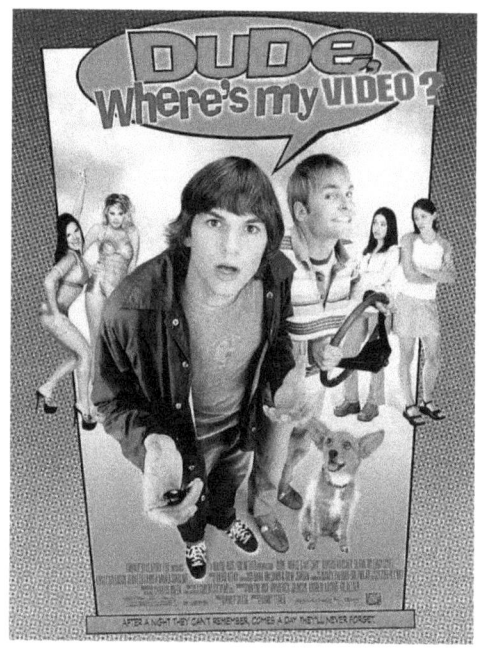

Still, nothing quite matched the satisfaction of deliberately mishearing a customer's order and sending them home with the exact opposite film to the one they wanted. Case in point: it didn't matter which one of these you asked for, you were getting the other one...

And to the child whose parents tried renting them the Cuba Gooding Jnr movie, Snow Dogs... you're welcome.

Don't take my wife... please!

LEARN STAND UP COMEDY / COPE WITH THE LOSS OF YOUR ABDUCTED WIFE

Want to know the secret of making an audience laugh? Struggling to deal with the brutal kidnap of a spouse? Then this is the course for you!

In this uniquely comprehensive course you'll learn the craft of joke writing, as well as coping with the trauma of your significant other being filed missing/presumed dead. You'll explore misdirection, structure, and rhythm while doing your utmost to blot out the memory of your beloved being chloroformed and bundled roughly into the back of a 2010 Polo Sedan.

Discover the Art of the Perfect One-Liner!

> A horse walks into a bar. The barman says "why the long face?" The horse says "because my wife was abducted and the chances of her showing up alive at this point are razor thin."

Take Inspiration From Your Life!

> You know when you get a phone call in the middle of the night and there's a modulated voice on the other end telling you that if ever want to see your wife again you'll go to the south west corner of Hyde park and leave a briefcase full of unmarked bills in the bin with the painted cross on it, but then when you get there all you find is your wife's severed finger and a note that says "this is for getting the police involved"? You don't? Good for you. Cherish your loved ones.

BOOK EARLY!!!

Sign up today and feel that toxic sense of despair melt away. Laughter is the best medicine, even if the love of your life was spirited away by rough-handed captors, leaving in her stead a pit that couldn't be filled with all the tears in the world !!!!!!!!!!!!

DAVID BUSSELL

Mad Men 1980s: Guess Who?

Thanks for stopping by gentlemen, please, take a bean bag. Can I get you a drink? Vodka? Martini? Old Fashioned? Hey, it's gotta be noon somewhere, right? No takers? Okay, just a round of Soda Streams then; Allison, be a peach and get busy with the fizzy, would you? Top mine off with a jigger of rye too, there's a gal.

I don't want to take up too much of your time today, boys, so I'll keep this brief. 'Guess Who?' What is it? One might describe it as "a little box of magic"... thank you, but please, still your applause – that quite brilliant and wholly sufficient tagline is merely the opening salvo in my war on your hearts and minds. It's cute, sure, but you didn't sign on this company's senior level closer for "cute," did you? The answer is a very senior "no."

Yes, enjoy my little joke before I skillfully divert what seems like casual patter into an affecting and thought-provoking commentary on our lives and times.

Boys, I'm going to be honest and say I don't think you've the faintest idea of what you're sitting on here, and I'm going to get a pass for doing so simply because my remarkable charisma has already allowed me to slip beneath your bed sheets like some modern day incubus.

See, on the surface of things, Guess Who is just a child's game, yet scratch deeper and you'll find it's more. Much more. It's educational, it's strategic, it requires deductive reasoning... but more than that it is revolutionary. Yes, you heard right, gentlemen, but allow me to say that word one more time in my smoky, testosterone-flavored voice...

Revolutionary.

So what's the hot topic here? Is it gender? Could be; after all, with its male/female imbalance, doesn't your product teach us once and for all that women are less valuable than men? Or maybe there's a richer seam to mine, for instance, race. Maybe I want to light the powder-keg of black versus white and sell your game as an exercise in eliminating people based on their minority traits. That's fun for kids and adults.

But no, because I plan to dig deeper still and show you something you'd scarcely imagined possible See, I took your game home to my luxury penthouse and gave it to one of my grandchildren to see what she made of it. As we played, I imagined I was leading a casting session full of beautiful models, and each time I flipped down a face I saw myself ruthlessly weeding out another slab of human meat that failed to meet my exacting sexual specifications.

It was hilarious.

But, as befits my vexing personality, I was exhibiting a satisfied exterior yet boiling with inner turmoil. Maybe it was a signature spell of Don Draper moodiness or perhaps a melancholy brought on by my eighth tumbler of scotch, but I looked down and for a solitary moment I saw my face on that board. There I was among George and Alfred and Bill and Susan, and I asked myself not "what color is my hair?" or "what color are my eyes?" but "what is my place in this world?" What shape is my soul? WHO AM I?!

At this point I'd usually beg "pray silence" for my big finale, except I see I've already captivated you with my engaging and emotionally resonant prelude, so I'll simply offer this as your new tagline...

Guess Who?: "What Makes a Man?"

And if that doesn't do it, my name's not Dick Whitman. I mean Don Draper. Damn it.

First draft chat-up lines

1. You look so good, I want to tattoo your face onto my face.

2. You're giving me a raging heart-on.

3. If I could rearrange the alphabet I'd put 'U' and 'I' together... although that would mean a total teardown of the English language, leading to widespread confusion, particularly among those who rely on the alphabet for their profession, for instance librarians and nursery school teachers.

4. Did it hurt? When you fell from heaven? I'm guessing it did by your horribly misshapen head.

5. Girl, are you a virus? 'Cause I wanna stick you straight in the spam folder.

Terror flight!

For the last seven years I've been stealing airline safety cards and cutting out panels to make this collage. As a result, I estimate that somewhere in the region of 17,000 lives have been lost.

32 BUT... YOU'RE A HORSE

A.C.E.d it

Plenty of folks like to play the big man and enter the name "A.C.E." on video game high score tables, but too few have the discipline to take it to the next level...

Solipsistic wrestlers

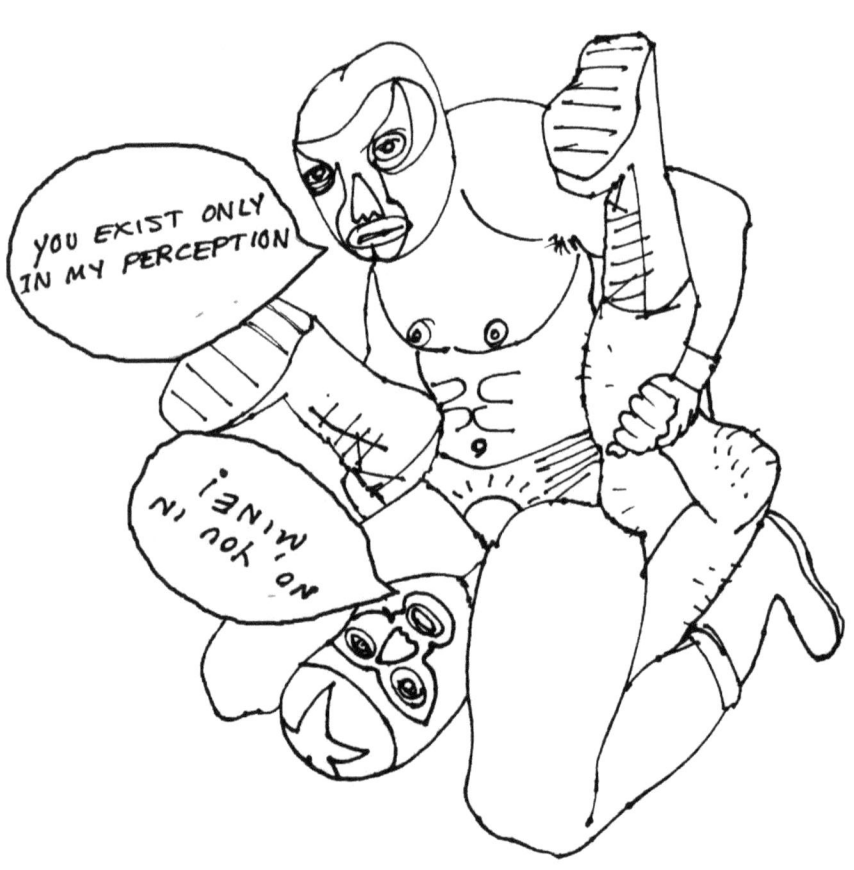

34 BUT... YOU'RE A HORSE

Fun with phones

The following is the result of me tinkering with the shortcut settings of my wife's iPhone...

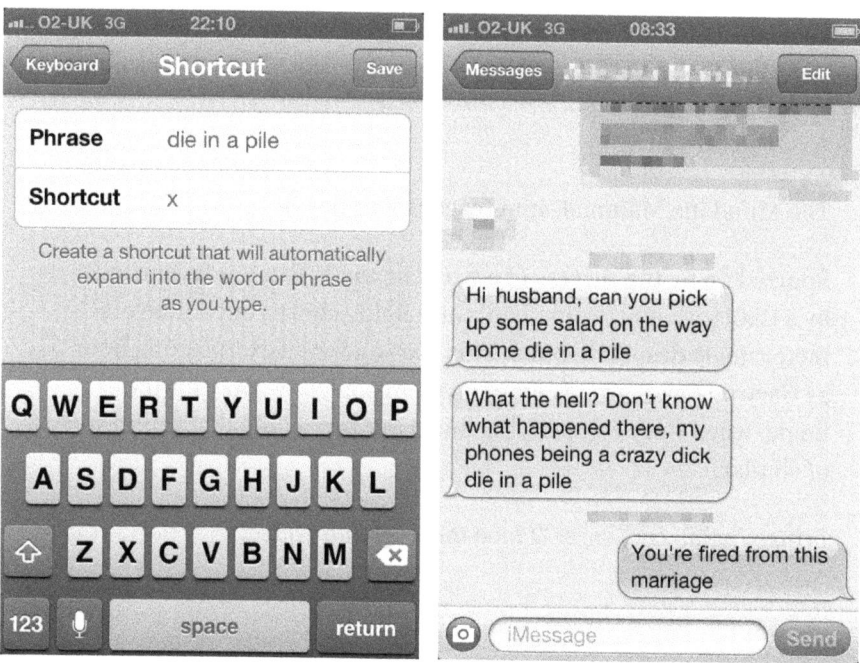

Top picks for the Fringe Festival

Paralysed with choice by this year's comedy festival line-up? Then let me be your guide to the best the fest has to offer with my Top 6 picks of the Fringe!

1. 'Puntification'

The Mundane Mammal, 1pm (except Tuesdays)

Spurred on by the success of a tweet he made that got favourited by a Cialis account, 'comedian' Gary Baldy churns out a litany of increasingly desperate puns. This goes on for an excruciating hour as Gary mistakes groans for enjoyment somehow. Stay for the finale, when Gary creates a big finish out two words that sound *sort of* similar.

FringeVagina.com says: *"I love the way that ended."*

2. **'Gag Girls'**

Downstairs at The Flailing Arms, 3pm

Be sure to arrive early to see these two hormone cases screaming "Come to our show! Come to our show!" at fellow comedians trying to enjoy their lunch. Marvel as they clamber aboard table tops, mashing their stiletto heels into people's food as they bark through gobs like fresh shotgun wounds in a last ditch attempt to persuade strangers to fill the yawning chasms of their empty souls.

A penis-shaped lollipop for anyone who brings along one of their flyers featuring them half-naked and airbrushed to within an inch of their lives.

3. **'Two Dudes in a Room'**

The Confused Uncle, 4pm

A pair of comics split and hour despite having nothing in common besides the fact they went halves on renting a flat. Flinch at the gearshift crunch between their wildly disparate acts! Witness the seething resentment still present from the evening before, when the tall one stole the little one's last Fondant Fancy! Stay for the end when the little one exacts revenge by skimming off the larger share of the donations bucket!

Chucklefucks says: *"I'm not laughing just thinking about it!"*

4. 'Cap'n Cock-a-Hoop's Fun-Time Imaginarium'

Wunder Bar, 2pm

Wacky prop comic Cap'n Cock-a-Hoop (who can be seen every morning handing out flyers dressed as a corn on the cob for no good fucking reason) conjures up a world of wonder more whimsical than a little French peasant girl tugging at a kite with her bottom lip sticking out.

The Scotchman says: *"Like watching a four year old running around with his dick super-glued to his elbow."*

5. 'Hair and Gone'

The Prole Hole, 10pm

Russell [insert surname here]; an asymmetrical haircut growing out of some tight trousers, leapfrogs over his debut hour on the way to a TV panel show. Catch him now while you're in spitting distance.

6. 'Serial Japist'

The Pensive Pony, 5pm (except Wednesdays)

A privileged twenty-something "shock comic" talks authoritatively on the subjects of sexual assault, paedophilia and AIDS, despite his biggest personal tragedy being the time he had to make an extra hole in his Prada belt because he'd been overdoing it at The Dorchester. Be sure to visit a second time after he's become fed up with no one laughing and rebranded his show as 'spoken word'.

ComedyRadar.co.uk says: *"About as edgy as a beach ball."*

All-purpose phrases I find useful when I have absolutely no idea what I'm talking about

1. Swings and roundabouts, isn't it?
2. It's a rich tapestry.
3. That's what I'm saying... ostensibly
4. It's all relative really.
5. Well, you have to these days.
6. It's the human condition
7. It is what it is.
8. That's Cameron's Britain for you...

Cats for the blind

A dog is your friend for life. A cat is a furry serial killer you buy dinner for. If you're injured around a dog it will fetch help. If you're injured around a cat it will wander around a bit until you die, then eat your face. This is why dogs are empirically better than cats. As further proof, there are no such things as cats for the blind. A guide dog is so loyal it can be taught to defecate on command. Attempting to teach a cat the same will lead to this...

Charged with looking after a blind person, this next cat has lured the afflicted man into an ambush of lions. And just look how happy she is about it! For shame, kitty.

This can't be safe...

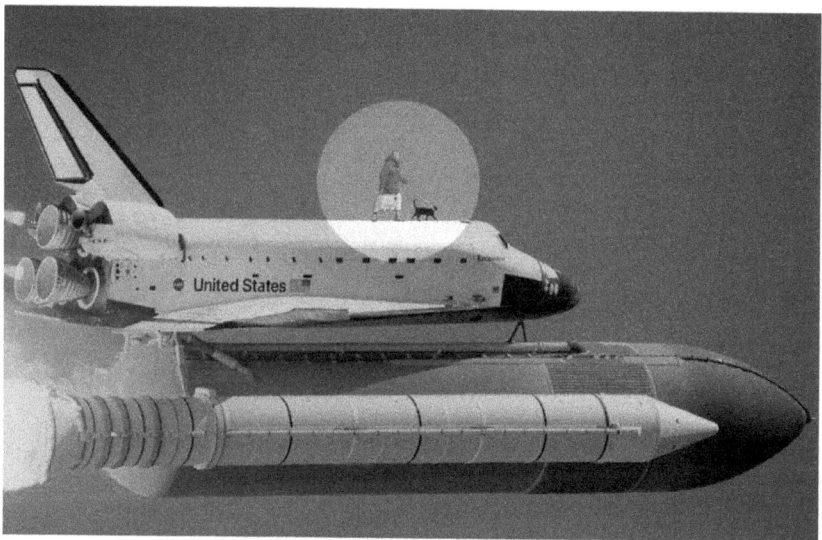

... and leading Mr Cohen this way is surely asking for trouble...

But wait, let's take a closer look...

42 BUT... YOU'RE A HORSE

Knock Knock hijack: Part two

Action movie crossovers for the equal opportunities era

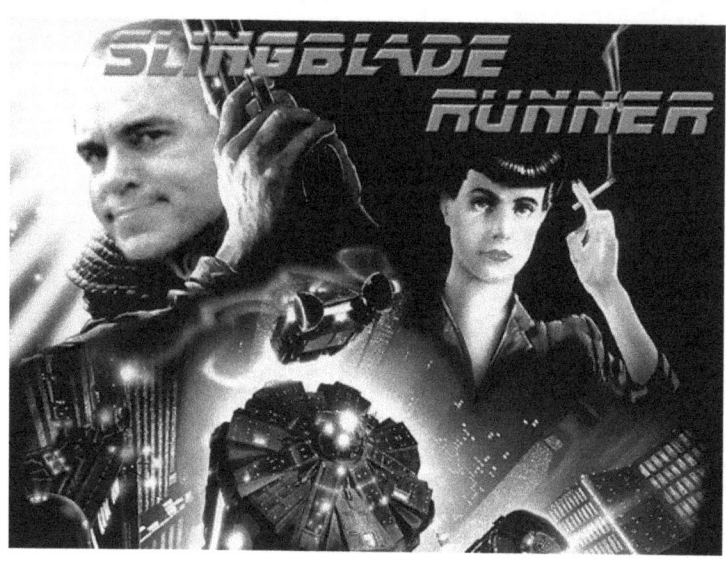

DAVID BUSSELL

Selling a haunted house

Last Halloween the wife and I put our house on the market. As a promotional stunt I thought it would be a canny move to have the listing feature a photo of a creepy ventriloquist dummy in every room. The wife had doubts, but I convinced her it was a good idea by using a time-honoured combination of bitching and getting my own way. What follows is a chain of email correspondence between myself and a potential buyer...

46 BUT... YOU'RE A HORSE

From: Douglas ▓▓▓▓
Date: Saturday 2 November 2013 11:46
To: David Bussell
Subject: 1 bed flat

Hi. We really like the look of your flat but my girlfriend wants to know what the story is with the dummy. Why is there a dummy in all the photos?

Doug

....

From: David Bussell
Date: Saturday 2 November 2013 13:22
To: Douglas ▓▓▓▓
Subject: Re: 1 bed flat

Dear Douglas

Thanks for being in touch. Sorry about the dummy. I swear the photos were clean when I posted them - he must have showed up later. He does that sometimes.

If you'd like to arrange a viewing I'm available most evenings and weekends, just let me know.

David

....

From: Douglas ▓▓▓▓
Date: Saturday 2 November 2013 14:02
To: David Bussell
Subject: Re Re: 1 bed flat

What do you mean he showed up later?

....

From: David Bussell
Date: Saturday 2 November 2013 14:54
To: Douglas ▓▓▓▓
Subject: Re: Re: Re: 1 bed flat

Dear Dougy

Just ignore the dummy. Worst impulse buy I ever made, that thing. You know how it is though, they put it by the till and you just have to have it, don't you?

Shall I pencil you in for a viewing Wednesday night?

....

From: Douglas ~~~~~
Date: Saturday 2 November 2013 15:12
To: David Bussell
Subject: Re Re: Re: Re: 1 bed flat

Why don't you just get rid of it if you don't want it?

Sorry, I have plans Wednesday.

....

From: David Bussell
Date: Saturday 2 November 2013 15:59
To: Douglas ~~~~~
Subject: Re: Re: Re: Re: 1 bed flat

Dear Dougables

Don't you think I've tried getting rid of it? First time my wife saw the thing she made me throw it out with the rubbish. The next day there it was though – sat right back on the shelf looking down at us with those laughing eyes.

How about Thursday?

....

From: Douglas ~~~~~
Date: Saturday 2 November 2013 16:18
To: David Bussell
Subject: Re Re: Re: Re: Re: 1 bed flat

Um ok.

Thursday could work. Question – would you be open to including the bookshelves in the sale – we really like them.

....

From: David Bussell
Date: Saturday 2 November 2013 15:59
To: Douglas ~~~~~
Subject: Re: Re: Re: Re: Re: Re: 1 bed flat

Dear Dougso

Of course. With one condition. You take the dummy too.

....

From: Douglas ~~~~~
Date: Sunday 3 November 2013 10:55
To: David Bussell
Subject: Re Re: Re: Re: Re: Re: Re: 1 bed flat

Thanks, but we really we don't really need that

....

From: David Bussell
Date: Sunday 3 November 2013 15:59
To: Douglas
Subject: Re: Re: Re: Re: Re: Re: Re: Re: 1 bed flat

Dear Dig Doug,

You probably made the right choice there. The thing's a menace. Can you believe I woke up to use the toilet last night and found this? Honestly, people say having a baby's tough but they don't know the half of it!

Attached image: FearingForMyLife.jpg

From: Douglas
Date: Sunday 3 November 2013 16:36
To: David Bussell
Subject: Re Re: Re: Re: Re: Re: Re: Re: Re: 1 bed flat

Is that meant to be funny?

From: David Bussell
Date: Sunday 3 November 2013 18:34
To: Douglas
Subject: Re Re: Re: Re: Re: Re: Re: Re: Re: Re:1 bed flat

Dear Douglish,

It's not my idea of funny, but then I'm more of a '2 Broke Girls' kind of guy. I tell you what definitely isn't funny, and that's flicking through old photos only to find the evil ventriloquist's dummy you own has been following you around since before you even bought him!

Attached images: Holiday.jpg, OfficeXmasParty.jpg, Wedding.jpg

....

From: Douglas
Date: Sunday 3 November 2013 18:42
To: David Bussell
Subject: Re Re: Re: Re: Re: Re: Re: Re: Re: Re: Re: 1 bed flat

Hi. Sorry, we put an offer on another place.

....

From: David Bussell
Date: Sunday 3 November 2013 19:10
To: Douglas
Subject: Re Re: Re: Re: Re: Re: Re: Re: Re: Re: Re:1 bed flat

Dear Duggles

Are you sure I can't persuade you? How about if I throw in one of these? Word to the wise: the guy I bought it from said to keep it well away from water.

Attached image: FuzzyFriend.jpg

[end of communication]

Sample reviews from Potpourri Monthly

"An epic, roaring avalanche of a potpourri... more, I want more!"

"If you only buy one potpourri this autumn, make it this one."

"Inventive. Idiomatic. Breathtakingly ambitious. In a perfect world this potpourri would be a compulsory purchase."

"Arguably one of the greatest potpourris of the 21st century."

"A stunning debut; I was laughing and crying by the first sniff."

He is risen!

DAVID BUSSELL

Top Wasp

A lot of you won't remember this, but Top Cat wasn't always known by that name. The original title for the popular Hanna-Barbera cartoon wasn't "Top Cat" at all, but "Top Wasp".

Hanna-Barbera even went so far as to produce a Top Wasp TV pilot, though the feedback from their test audience was less than positive. The choice of giving the lead to a venomous pest was considered ill-judged, plus audience members complained they couldn't make out the protagonist's dialogue over the sound of his incessant buzzing.

They also said they found it hard to understand why a winged invertebrate was friends with so many cats, as illustrated by the front cover of this Top Wasp comic...

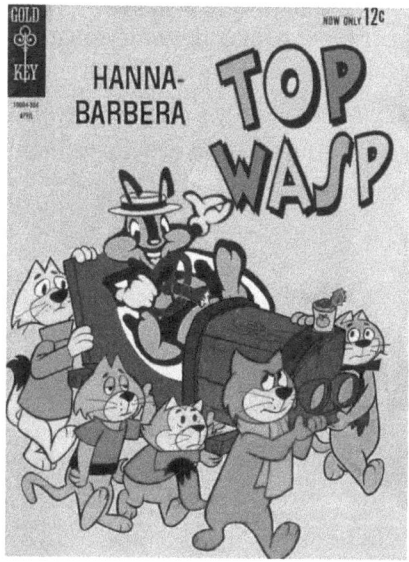

Another objection to the pilot was its ending, wherein Top Wasp murdered Officer Dibble with an injection of potent toxin into his brain stem...

DAVID BUSSELL 57

The general consensus was that it cut short a promising dynamic between the two characters. Others complained about the incredibly graphic nature of the assassination, which included a lingering close-up of Dibble frothing at the gums as he lay dying in a filthy back alley upon a carpet of broken hypodermics.

Of course Top Wasp isn't the only example of a pilot falling foul of the "wasp protagonist" trap, as anyone who remembers the original iteration of this show will attest...

Photoshop tools I wish I could use on my memories of being a teenager

Things to do today

Date _____

Priority   Dealt with

① UNDO _____ ○
② EXTRACT _____ ○
③ ADD NOISE _____ ○
④ PURGE _____ ○
⑤ BLUR MORE _____ ○
○ _____ ○
○ _____ ○

Mad Men 1980s: Rubik's Cube

Thanks for stopping by, Mister Rubik, what brings you to the office of Don Draper? I see; may I have a closer look at your prototype? Fascinating. Beautifully crafted, intricate – you've managed to achieve the impossible and create a piece of art that's *actually* enjoyable.

Check it out, I completed a side.

Let me ask you though, is it possible to cheat this puzzle of yours? I see. Yes, I suppose you could peel off the stickers... the same way a man might peel away the layers of his conscience in order to engage in a string of sexual infidelities that errode his soul until he's little more than an impression of a human being.

That's the greens done.

How about you tell me some more about this cube of yours? What's that? "Forty three quintillion wrong answers but only a single correct one?" Reminds me of some discussions I've had with my former wives! Amiright? Come on, pal, don't leave this thing unfived.

Something that concerns me though - that accent of yours – where does the name Rubik come from? Hungary you say? Oh boy, there's a wrinkle. The Soviet Union's a real hard sell right now, what with Reagan in the White House and the whole Cold War thing. Never mind though, because I'm about to hit you up with a tagline so powerful it'll smash a hole right through the Berlin Wall.

Rubik's Cube: "Not Just a Communist Block."

And that's the last side complete. How about that, I solved your little puzzle *and* cooked up a pitch perfect promotional strategy for it. Boy, I truly am the mack daddy of the ad racket.

Oxymoron

As a man who grew to maturity without contracting Bieber Fever (likewise Achy Breaky Heart and the Boogaloo Flu) I have precious little knowledge of the Canadian singer nor what it is he has against music. One of the few things I do know is that he appeared in a movie that somehow managed, in three short words, to contradict itself twice...

What a pickle. If only there were some way to honour the sentiment of the original title <u>and</u> fix the glaring oxymoron. But could such a thing be possible?

Boy, you better Beliebe it!

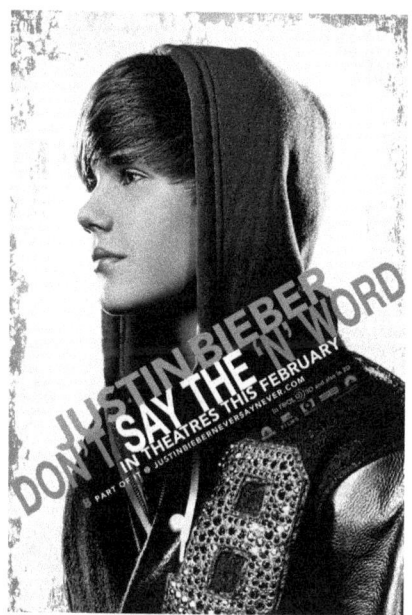

Megaphone City

Telephone transcript dated 2nd November 2013, 15:43

ME: Hello, is this Megaphone City?

MEGAPHONE CITY: Yes, sir.

ME: I wonder if you can help me - do you stock the Monacor TM-5399?

MEGAPHONE CITY: Say again, please.

ME: The Monacor TM-5399?

MEGAPHONE CITY: No, sir, we don't have that model.

ME: How about the PYLE PMP40 Professional?

MEGAPHONE CITY: I'll just check with a colleague. One moment... (goes away and returns) ...no, we don't stock that either. We've got Nokia, Samsung, Motorola...

ME: ...do any of them come with an external jack for a 12 volt battery?

MEGAPHONE CITY: Let me just check... (goes away for a long time) ...hello? No I don't see that listed under any of our accessories.

ME: Okay. How about built-in anti howl?

MEGAPHONE CITY: Doesn't look like...

ME: ...waistband amp and carry strap?

MEGAPHONE CITY: No.

ME: Siren function?

MEGAPHONE CITY: Siren? Like a ringtone?

ME: Ringtone? I'm looking for a loud hailer, not a mobile phone.

MEGAPHONE CITY: Um, we don't sell loud hailers.

ME: I'm sorry, is this not Megaphone City?

MEGAPHONE CITY: Yes, but...

ME: How could your shop be called Megaphone City if you don't sell megaphones?

MEGAPHONE CITY: No, it's mega phone, like mega phones.

ME: Megaphones, yes.

MEGAPHONE CITY: No... mega like great. Great phones.

ME: Oh, so there's a space between mega and phone?

MEGAPHONE CITY: ...yes... that's right.

ME: Oh my God, I'm so sorry, I was under the impression the "megaphone" on your shop front was one word. What a turd.

MEGAPHONE CITY: It's okay...

ME: ...here I am banging on about megaphones, when all the while I've been talking to a man who sells *mega phones*. Talk about sticking my dick in it.

MEGAPHONE CITY: Er, that's fine...

ME: It's not fine. If I'd actually read the sign on the front of your shop that <u>definitely</u> says Mega Phone <u>with a space</u>, I wouldn't have wasted your time like this. What a sub-human shit! I've had enough - one more cock-up I said – one more cock-up and I'm going to do the world a favour and get off this merry-go-round for good. Well, goodbye, friend. Goodbye forever!

MEGAPHONE CITY: It's really not—

ME: (Hangs up).

(56 seconds later)

ME: Hello.

MEGAPHONE CITY: Megaphone City, how can I help you?

ME: (Extremely loudly, though a megaphone) DO YOU HAVE THE NEW NOKIA?

MEGAPHONE CITY: (Hangs up)

[End of communication]

Tragic Google searches

Can I get a refund on a rape whistle?

How to remove Buzz Lightyear toy from anus after wings activate

2 Broke Girls blooper reel

Dean Gaffney erotic fiction

Bing

Bussfeed

Three Telltale Sins You Were Born In The 80s

Step aside, '90s kids!

1. Your birth certificate lists the year of your DOB as being from 1980 to 1989.

2. Your passport lists the year of your DOB as being from 1980 to 1989.

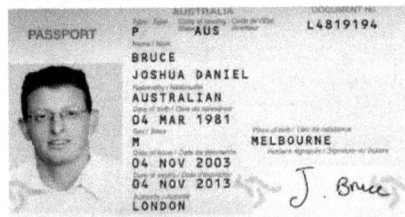

3. Your attested court order containing a raised court seal that includes your full name (examples being an adoption document, a name change document, and a gender change document) lists the year of your DOB as being from 1980 to 1989.

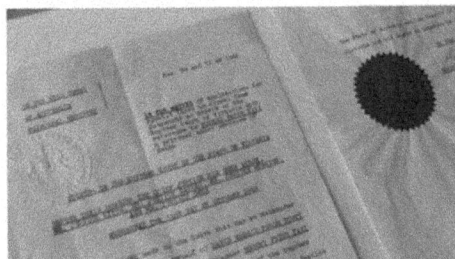

Twerk to the Future

A bloke's guide to lip balm

It's a question for the ages: how does a man apply lip balm in public without feeling like he's eating a banana in front of a builder with both hands tied behind his back?

It's taken decades of intensive research, but after three failed marriages, a crippling drug addiction and a day trip to Alton Towers, I finally have the solution. Gentlemen and regular men, I give you the six-step guide to putting on lip balm without sacrificing your masculinity...

1. Extract lip balm from pocket

Draw in one swift motion, like it's high noon and you're a gunslinger pulling his six-shooter on a ruthless cattle baron.

2. Remove cap

Flick it off like a gun safety. It's time to go to battle; you are Godzilla and your lips... are that really crappy Nineties remake of Godzilla.

3. Brandish

Proudly! No hiding your light under a Bussell (as the expression goes), hold that thing aloft like it's a torch and you're running the final stretch of an Olympic relay.

4. Apply to knuckles

Finesse forbidden. Slap that shit on like Yves Kline transforming a naked lady into a living paint brush. Wait a second, you're aware of leading proponent of Nouveau réalisme, Yves Kline? We're in full-blown gay panic mode here, you frou-frou freak, go back to Step 1 and start over!

5. Punch face

No holding back, take your fist balm and crack yourself in the goddamned mouth.

6. Marinade in applause

Congratulations, you did it, you weather-proofed your kisser without looking like a big fat ovary. Now high five yourself until your hands catch on fire.

Halloween costume ideas

Stuck for a Halloween costume? Here are some spooky suggestions that will guarantee you're the toast of the party!

Frank-Einstein:
E=MC Scared!

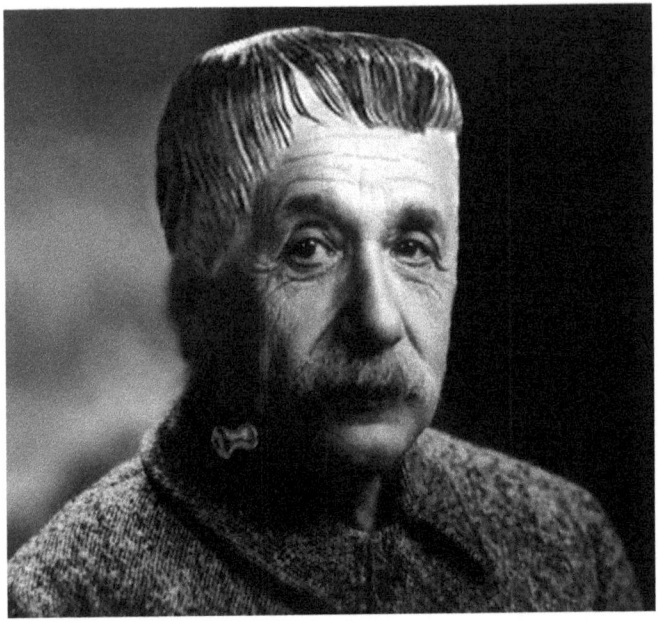

The Blur:
Mess with your host's photos by arriving in one quarter resolution.

The Mike Myers/Michael Myers Confusion:
Psycho-delic, baby!

Scarecase:

From the 1986 Horror, 'Scarecase'. Described by Fangoria magazine as "nastier than a blackface Gary Glitter".

Blackface Gary Glitter:

See previous.

Steven Haunting:
robot voice "The Phantom... of... the... opera...........
is....................................here."

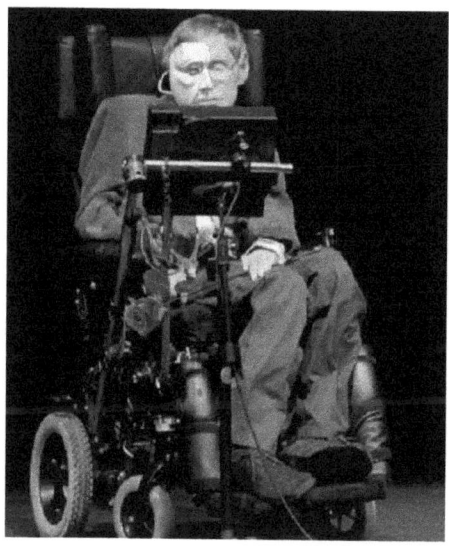

Handyman:
Dare you say his name into a mirror three times?

CHOOSE YOUR OWN ADVENTURE
YOU'RE THE STAR OF THE STORY! CHOOSE MANY POSSIBLE ENDINGS.
XXX SORORITY GIRLS GONE WILD!!!

Greetings, carnal adventurer, and welcome to the challenge of your sexual lifetime! Will you be able to stop frotting your junk long enough to reach the shuddering climax of this erotic quest? Head to the next page to find out...

76 BUT... YOU'RE A HORSE

Welcome to **XXX Sorority Girls Gone Wild**, where anything is possible. Are you ready to begin?

No. 1
Yes. 2

1

Pleased with your decision not to waste the day reading amateur pornography, you head to the library to borrow the complete works of E.M. Forster. Unfortunately, your snooty nose is held so high that you fail to spot an open manhole, which causes you to tumble face-first into a sewer and contract a lethal infection. Within less than 24 hours you are dead from septic shock. **GAME OVER.**

2

Great. Now let's decide who you are and what you're into. First things first, are you a boy or a girl?

I'm a Girl. 3
I'm a Boy. 4

DAVID BUSSELL 77

3

That's ridiculous. Return to 1 and **TRY AGAIN.**

4

Good for you, kiddo. So, how many hot ladies do you think you can handle?

Just the one, thanks.	5
Two, maybe seventy-two?	6

5

Unfortunately, your limp, sissy wrist is so weak that you drop your decaf coffee into your lap and burn your penis to a scarred little nub. There will be no XXX action for you. **GAME OVER.**

6

Now we're talking! Tall order for one guy though. Might be you could use more than the one dick. How many dicks would you like to have?

I can make do with the one, bro.	7
As many dicks as you can throw at me!	8

7

Great, let's get started!

You're a hot young buck looking for a good time and you know just where to find it. You ring the doorbell of the local chapter house to be greeted by a sorority girl in an itsy-bitsy crop top who looks like she could solve a Rubik's Cube with her ass. Beyond her are a group of girls so smoking you could cook hot pockets between their cans.

The girl at the door says "hello?" What do you say back?

Present a stack of pizzas. "Which of you ladies is the meat lover?"   9
Thumb to your pussy wagon. "Wanna take a ride in the f*ck truck?"   10
Show her your toolbox. "I'm here to check out your plumbing."   11

8

A child of Chernobyl, you were exposed in the womb to dangerous levels of mutagenic radiation. The fallout from the disaster caused a scrambling of your genetic blueprint, leading you to be born with an excess of genitalia. Unfortunately, as a citizen of the Ukraine, you live nowhere near any sorority houses (XXX or otherwise), and because of your condition you die aged six of acute thyroid cancer. **GAME OVER.**

DAVID BUSSELL   79

9

The girl says "about time" and asks where her pizza is. You hand over the goods and she chides you for your tardiness, reminding you that Papa Pepperoni has a '30 Minutes Or Your Pizza Free' policy. As she closes the door, you curse your ambiguousness before climbing back onto your scooter. On your return trip to the restaurant you lament the unnecessary cost to your employer, Papa Pepperoni, a kind old man who treats you like the son he never had. Unfortunately, the distraction causes you to miss a stop sign and you wind up sandwiched between two speeding trucks. You die in agony, a disc of flattened flesh and bone. **GAME OVER.**

10

The girl says "you betcha" and throws on a coat. Having climbed into your automobile, it becomes immediately apparent that she has somehow failed to process the "f*ck" part of your request. Thanking you for your generosity, she asks if you wouldn't mind swinging by the Glendale Galleria so she can pick up some shopping. Several hours pass before she returns to the vehicle, claiming she's tired and would like to go home. Having dropped her back at the chapter house, you run out of gas on the way to your apartment and are forced to hitch a ride. Unfortunately, the driver turns out to be the notorious "screwdriver stabber" and your body is found on an interstate shoulder two days later, perforated by an eight-piece Black and Decker tool set. **GAME OVER.**

11

The girl smiles and invites you inside, introducing you to the rest of her hot sorority sisters. You are about to open your zipper when she directs you to the kitchen sink and explains that the drain has been backed up all week. She says she thinks it's a simple enough fix. "Just use your big tool and loosen those nuts". How do you respond?

"Speaking of big tools…"   12
"Speaking of loose nuts…"   13
"Would you ladies care for some sex?"   14

12

"Yes…?" she says, eyeing you quizzically. Eventually you decide you'd better do something, so you head out to your truck to fetch a toolbox, only you're too ashamed to return and drive home instead. Taking a good look at yourself in the bathroom mirror that night, you come to realize you don't like what you see there anymore. Stepping into a hot bath, you draw a razor blade across a vein and slip forever into sweet oblivion. **GAME OVER.**

13

"Yes, the nuts need loosening so the waste pipe can be detached and the blockage removed" the girl says. After a long pause you decide you'd better get on with the job, and begin unscrewing the nut with your fingers. Unfortunately, without use of the proper tool, you slip and lacerate your wrist on a loose screw. Death from shock and blood loss is almost instantaneous. **GAME OVER.**

14

The girl gasps and says "pardon me?!" The entire sorority turns, arms folded. What would you like to do now?

Say "I said, have you ladies seen my specs?"	15
Feign a stroke.	16
Repeat your original question.	17

15

By co-incidence, one of the sisters happens to find a pair of glasses and asks "are these yours?" Pretending they are, you thank her and put them on. Unfortunately, they're not made out to your prescription, rendering you practically blind. Groping for the sink, you place your hand in the drain in an effort to remove the clog, but accidentally locate the waste disposal unit instead. The blades whir to life, chewing your hand off at the wrist. Death from shock and blood loss is almost instantaneous. **GAME OVER.**

16

You cross your eyes and go limp, but manage to strike your head on the corner of the kitchen island during your journey to the floor. The blunt force trauma is so fierce it causes one of your eyeballs to dislodge from your skull, and the resulting neurological complications consign you to a wheelchair for what remains of your short life. **GAME OVER.**

17

The girls say "fine" and you have some sex and it's great (please masturbate accordingly). **THE END.**

Manly things I have yet to do

1. Crawl through an air duct.
2. Outrun a fireball.
3. Re-load a gun before the spent cartridge hits the floor.
4. Throw a sheriff's badge into the sand.
5. Hurl a man into a jet engine.
6. Eat a peach with a dagger.
7. Throw a fallen comrade's dog tags into the ocean.
8. Yell "TAKE THE WHEEL!" at a passenger before climbing onto the hood to fight a terrorist.
9. Punch a hole through a wall next to a person's head I'd really like to punch but it goes against my moral code to do so.
10. Exercise.

There can be only mum

FOUR WALLS AND A FUCK SWING

Featured on
Captain Kangaroo
CBS-TV

MAKE HER YOURS WITH THIS ONE SIMPLE TRICK

Roses? Chocolates? A complex yet stable personality? Fools gold, one and all! If you really want to snag a mate you only need five things: **four walls and a fuck swing!**

Let's say you meet the lady of your dreams and talk her into coming back to your place. Good for you! But what's the first thing she sees when she walks through your door? Furniture. Appliances. Some pet. Are we feeling sexy yet? **No siree!**

Here's what you do: take your couch, your stereo, your dog, take them all outside and set them on fire. **Your bed too.** *"But won't I need my bed?"* you say. Pop a squat a listen up, sport, you've got a lot to learn.

You're in it to seal the deal, right? Darn tootin' you are, so write that deal in **plain English**. A bed sends mixed signals. You can make whoopie in a bed, but you can sleep there too. **Don't give her a Plan B, give her a fuck swing!** You ever hear of anyone sleeping on a fuck swing? No you haven't. Ever hear of someone talking about their *"feelings"* on a fuck swing? Never happened. **Not once in the history of the world has that happened.**

$49.99¢ in most stores

FOUR WALLS AND A FUCK SWING IT'S ALL YOU NEED!

Erotic minutes

Occasionally, very occasionally, I'm required to expend energy at my place of work, most notably when I'm called upon to minute committee meetings. Not to be melodramatic about it, but it's a task I relish about as much as wiring fish hooks to the ceiling, swallowing those fish hooks, then throwing myself down a lift shaft.

But what if committee meetings got sexy? What if the debates weren't the only thing in the room that were turgid? What if the participants cared less about public sector pay freezes and zero-hours contracts, and more about the animal calling of their frothing loins?

190/10

October

To
From   David Bussell
Agenda item   3.1
For   Information
Subject   Unconfirmed minutes of Pay Negotiations update 5 July 2013

Present   Alice ▓▓▓ (Chair)
              Rory ▓▓▓
              Tracey ▓▓▓
              Mariette ▓▓▓
              Jason ▓▓▓

1. **Welcome and Apologies**

    1.1. The Chair welcomed the Committee to the meeting, noting that all members were present.

2. **Pay Negotiations**

    2.1. Rory ▓▓▓ updated the Committee on the state of play in regards to nationwide industrial action over pay and conditions.

    2.2. Mariette ▓▓▓ ran a hand coquettishly through her flame-red hair. Congratulating Rory on the success of the campaign, she reported that it had been "*huge in* [her] *sector*"; a double-entendre she gave further emphasis to by lasciviously crossing and uncrossing her milk-white thighs.

2.3. Tracey ▓▓▓ bristled. For a while now she and Rory had been enjoying the private pleasure of one another's company, partaking of sun-dappled luncheons beneath orchard trees and flirtatious sojourns along the banks of England's enchanting brooks. Tracey knew she had no real claim to Rory given that he had yet to formally declare himself her beau, but still, Mariette's pernicious intrusions were quite beyond the pale.

2.4. Mariette sensed Tracey's umbrage and smiled as she loosened the top button of her blouse. Leaning forward to accentuate her décolletage, she cast a surreptitious glance at Rory's nether regions before expressing concerns over his "*growing* [work]*load*" and suggesting he and she find time to "*explore the mounting action at Congress*".

2.5. Despite his affections for his darling Tracey, Rory couldn't help but respond physically to Marianne's honeyed words. Shifting in his seat, he gulped audibly and replied that he would certainly "*welcome any help to ease the pressure*", then flushed rose pink at the unintended duality of his chosen figure of speech.

2.6. Tracey shot Mariette a wicked look. This was so like her, to make eyes at another's suitor! It had been this way ever since they had attended Lady Grace's finishing school together, and Mariette had led astray the vicar's son. Well, not this time! Tracey would see to it that Mariette's efforts to bewitch her man were in vain. Lightly brushing Rory's hand with hers, so gently as to seem accidental, she engaged Rory in a manner befitting of a lady, complimenting him on the ease in which her sector had been able to mobilise around his strategy.

2.7. Rory felt a spark of electricity as Tracey's velvety flesh grazed his own, and as they locked eyes he felt his sap *rise* ever further. Still, he was torn, dragged like a moth to the flame by the creamy orbs of Mariette's heaving bosom.

2.8. Sensing victory, Marianne threw back her head aimed a throaty laugh at the sky (or at least the polystyrene tiles of the meeting room's suspended ceiling).

2.9. Jason ▓▓▓ reported on the implementation of national pay scales in the North West, which had led to a non-consolidated offer of 0.2%, but nobody gave a fresh fig what Jason had to say.

2.10. Tracey knew she must fight fire with fire in order to combat Mariette's scandalous advances. Slipping off a peach-coloured suede moccasin, she slyly extended a Primark stockinged foot under the table, letting it land gently on the pulsating warmth of Rory's loins.

2.11. Rory yielded to Tracey's touch, fire igniting within his soul as his engorged member strained violently against the corduroy prison of his britches.

2.12. Sensing a worthy challenge to her wanton provocations, Mariette advanced the game to match point, placing a Biro bearing the slogan 'Fair Pensions for All' betwixt her cherry-red lips and suggestively working around the nib with her nimble tongue.

2.13. Not to be outdone, Tracey continued to work her foot up and down Rory's shaft, caressing his glands exquisitely with adroit manipulations of her delicate toes.

2.14. Feeling himself about to reach crisis, Rory crossed his legs in a desperate attempt to stop the inevitable, but his efforts were for nought. He exploded in shuddering climax, the likes of which he hadn't felt since the close of his keynote speech to the 2007 Annual Sector Conference on Government Changes to the 14-19 Curriculum.

2.15. The Chair called for order, bringing the meeting to an early close as she used a sheaf of agenda items to fan furiously at the flames of her burning ardour.

THE MEETING CLOSED AT 13:30

R.I.P. Mrs Wayne

British sitcoms that sound like slang for defecation

1. Blackadder Goes Forth.
2. The Mighty Boosh.
3. Lead Balloon.
4. Lunch Monkeys
5. Drop the Dead Donkey.

Deep comedy

It had been a typical evening of stand up comedy until the prop comic arrived, heaving his sack of home-made junk onto the stage to a ghost of an applause. He lurched into his routine regardless, but when his fifth joke flopped, something inside of him snapped. With great fury he began to bounce his props off the floor and snap them over his knee as he cursed and wailed at the crowd. What made the sight so remarkable, other than the fact he still had a tin of cat food stuck to his chin (WHISKAS!), is that prop comics are meant to be the fun guys of comedy. The gentle clowns. And yet there he was, Timmy Mallet biting Michaela Strachan on the face.

I can honestly say I've never laughed so much as I did at that prop comic suffering a complete mental breakdown. Because I support live comedy. That said, I can't be doing with stand up in quote form. I'm talking about those hyper-earnest black and white Facebook memes of Bill Hicks dressed like a gunslinger next to his "It's just a ride" quote, or George Carlin talking about how we're all made of recycled stars. The one your idiot friend posts to his timeline in an attempt at convincing people he's a man of profound thoughts. It's because of one such doorknob that I decided to retaliate with some cut-and-paste comedy wisdom of my own…

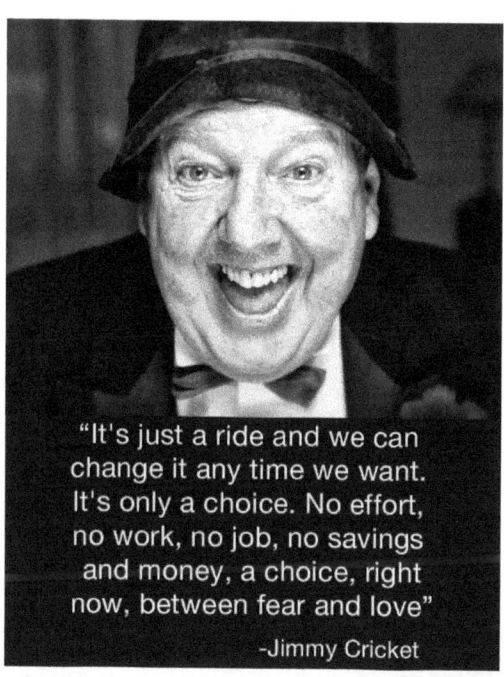

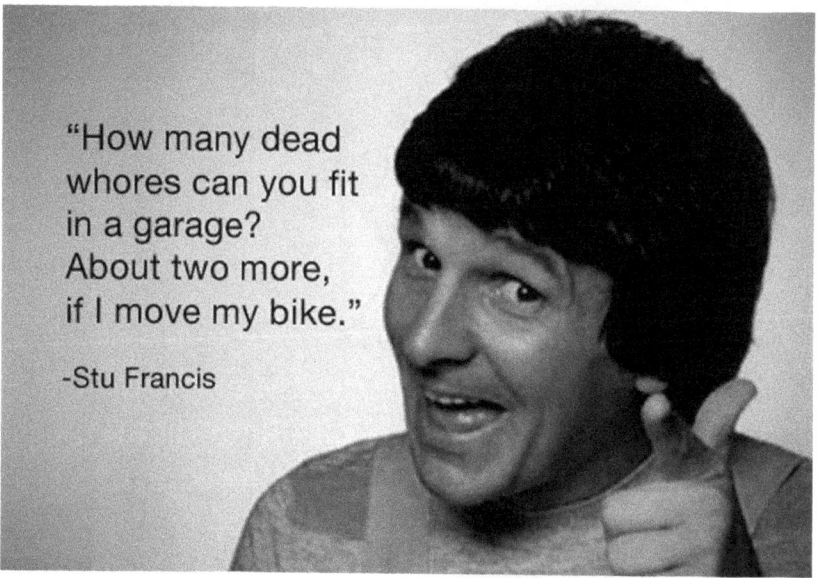

A three-legged dog walks into a saloon. He hops up to the bar and says: "I'm looking for the man who shot my paw."

-Bill Hicks

"If you're so pro-life, do me a favour: don't lock arms and block medical clinics. If you're so pro-life, lock arms and block cemeteries."

-Lenny Henry

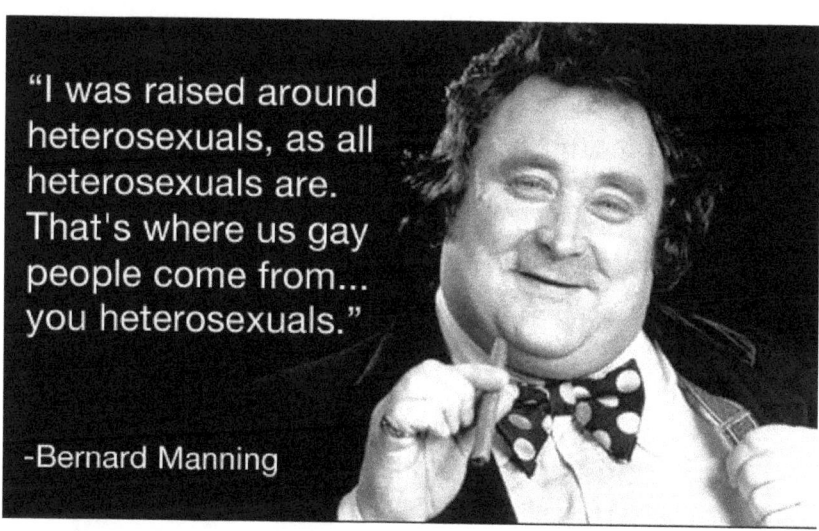

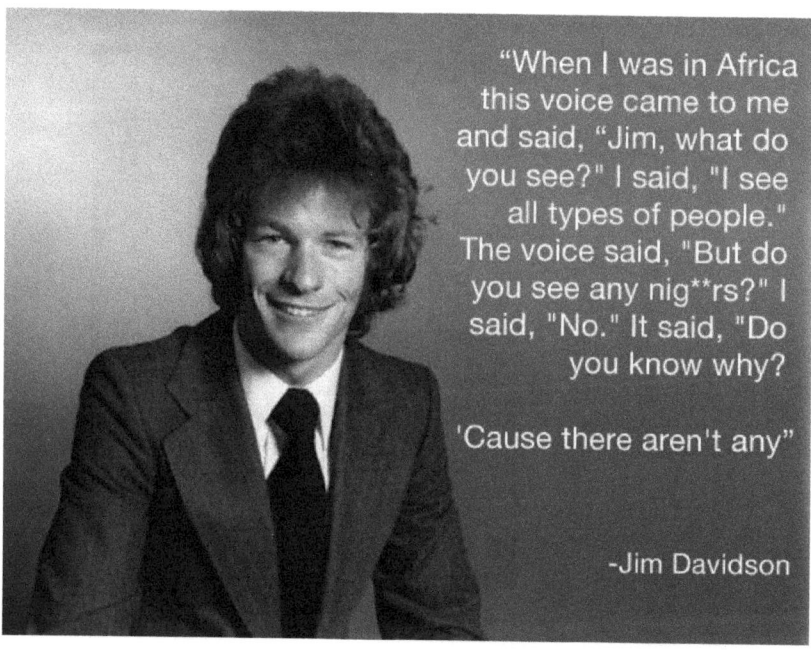

"You know what they say "There's no reason to ever hit a woman." Shit! There's a reason to hit everybody. You just don't do it. Shit, there's a reason to kick an old man down a flight of stairs. You just don't do it. Ain't nobody above an ass-whooping."
-Ronnie Corbett

"Garlic bread?!"

-George Carlin

Awesome pranks, AKA dick moves

Things to do today

1. Mail a friend a nude kiddie photo of yourself with the message 'ha ha, now you're a paedophile', because it's your body and you can do what you like with it.
2. Leave a piece of paper in the office copier that says 'Make Redundant?' and below it a shortlist of colleagues.
3. Write a message in Comic Sans. Make that message a graphic designer's obituary.
4. Make your outgoing voicemail message the exact sound of your phone ringing.
5. Next time you see someone on the street try turning a trip into a jog, catch up with them and keep pace until they're in the sea.
6. Propose to your fiancé by leaping out of her dead father's grave.
7. Borrow a friend's car then return it two weeks late and full to bursting with dead clowns.

DAVID BUSSELL

If, like millions of honest Americans, you make your living as a graphic designer for an animal pornography magazine, you'll know yours is a job fraught with pitfalls.

Anyone who works in an office knows the embarrassment of being caught goofing off. We've all found ourselves doing something we shouldn't during work hours, say balancing a shopping budget when we *should* be airbrushing images of grubby man-on-beast action, when suddenly... **RUMBLED!**

Instead of finalizing the layout of the February centerfold, you've been caught elbow-deep in a spreadsheet! Try wriggling out of that bucket of syrup!

But help is at hand, thanks to **Animal Porn Boss Screens**. Simply sign up to our internet web service and you'll have access to an unlimited gallery of emergency wallpapers. We've got everything you need all under one roof, from cows to coyotes, from sheep to squids, from lemurs to labradors – all sexually molested by a hardworking **APBS** employee.

So don't be caught napping - sign up today and never again fear the sound of your boss' footsteps!

APBS

Open an account during the week of January and we'll throw in a complimentary mouse mat **FREE OF CHARGE!**

I ♥ Bestiality

Special OFFER

---

100 BUT... YOU'RE A HORSE

Mad Men 1980s: Garbage Pail Kids

Shake my hand, sirs, it's a real honor to finally meet the bad boys of the collectable sticker world.

Ha, just look at these things; "Dressy Jesse"? A man in women's clothes, are you kidding me? How about this one, "Up Chuck" - reminds me of the time Roger ate all those oysters and the elevator went out. Boy, he went off like a ghetto fire hydrant! Or take this guy, "Adam Bomb" – that's some incendiary wit right there, linking the bomb to the Garden of Eden; the original big bang. Science meets religion, it's an explosion all of its own. What's that? Oh, Adam like "Atom." Okay, I didn't get that. Well, that takes it to a whole new level.

I don't need to tell you gents that what you've created here is a phenomenon. Your trading cards are being passed around classrooms faster than chicken pox. My own grandson (I forget which one) spends every red cent I give him on your stickers. He's so busy working on his collection that he's stopped paying attention in school altogether. I'm not kidding, the boy's dumb as a stump. His teacher, Miss Sanderson, called me in to discipline him on the matter, but... well, let's just say my son wasn't the only one who got disciplined that day!

I'm talking full sex.

But back to the reason you're here. It's no secret why your product is as successful as it is; your characters are irreverent, eye-catching and above all, hilarious. Your critics may call your product "gross" but they have it all wrong – Garbage Pail Kids don't work because they disgust us, they work because they celebrate the different... the rejects... the freaks. When I see "Slobby Robbie," or "Mauled Paul" I don't see a monster, I see a brother. I could do without "Rapin' Ron" though, that guy's pretty out there. Come again? Oh, it's pronounced "Rappin' Ron"? Then scratch that last part.

There's a lot of money being made here already, but you have to look after the long term. Sure, you've got the kids eating out of your hands now, but how do you make sure your product grows with your customer base? As long as your buyers are in the classroom, your cards are hot property, but what about when they get older? Think little Timmy's going to be interested in "Oozy Susie" when Floozy Susie, the next door neighbor his mother warned him about, comes knocking? Not likely. But don't sweat it, because I have the means to make sure little Timmy never, ever forgets his Garbage Pail friends.

DAVID BUSSELL

The secret... is in the glue.

I'm going to put you boys in touch with a factory that cooks a horse paste so strong it'll take the breath of Godzilla to get the damned things off. So when little Timmy's all grown up and Floozy Susie comes knocking, he won't be able to forget the Garbage Pail Kids, because they'll be right there, cemented to his bedroom door so fast he'd have to take the thing off its hinges and toss it in a volcano to get rid of them.

That, gents, is the ultimate definition of brand stickiness, and it's why your tagline can only be:

Garbage Pail Kids: "Trash You'll Treasure Forever."

Draper out!

downs scotch and spikes empty tumbler on the floor

PRIDE GARDENING

THE TRUE MEANING OF MANSCAPING!

Another British Summer, Another Hose Pipe Ban!

The grass is parched and your begonias are withering away, but don't worry, because help is at hand!

No matter the weather, we guarantee the downpour your garden needs, and it's all thanks to God's insatiable hatred of homosexuals! Just give us a call and we'll send a pair of gays to fornicate on your lawn in full view of the Creator.

In no time at all you'll have incurred His terrible wrath and your prize Hydrangea's will be in full bloom!

No job too big! Does your team's football pitch look like a cattle drive came through it? No problem, give us a call and we'll send you so many gays you'll think the parade came to town! They can't make babies, but they can sure as hell fertilise your lawn! *Call 01254 453873 and spit right in God's eye!*

DAVID BUSSELL

Baby on board

As a man, it often strikes me as unfair that the only type of "gimme yer seat" badge the London Underground offers is for expectant mothers. Surely there are complications besides pregnancy that warrant a bit of a sit down? I certainly think so, which is why I've begun designing a collection of badges that provide for a richer palette of human misery.

Why not cut out one of the illustrations from the following page, colour it in, and use your handy button-making kit to fashion a badge of your own? Because a joke's a joke and you have no intention of pissing away the infinitesimal sliver of human existence the universe gave you? Fair enough then.

Top Ten numbers

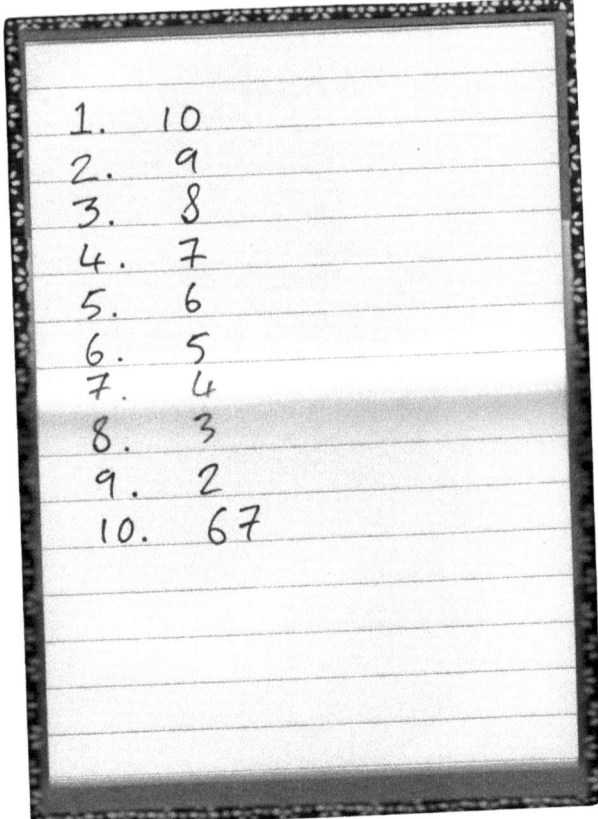

Knock Knock hijack: Part three

Steve
its monday morning so jokes time!
21 minutes ago via Facebook for Blackberry · Comment · Like

👍 7 people like this

> Steve knock knock..
> 21 minutes ago · Like

> David Who's there? Hello? Hello? Anybody? Damn it! That's enough, I've had all I can take of those lousy kids! *wires doorbell to the mains and waits*
> 20 minutes ago · Like · 👍 4

> Steve ure ruining this dave!!
> 19 minutes ago · Like

> Tim *whistling* Here I come, all ready to bring the Good News to another of God's flock. I'll just ring the doorbell and—ARRRGGHH! *collapses*
> 18 minutes ago · Like · 👍 4

> Steve Celeste
> 18 minutes ago · Like · 👍 1

David What the....? Oh no, I didn't really mean to hurt anyone!
17 minutes ago · Like · 👍 4

Steve CELESTE!!!
17 minutes ago · Like · 👍 3

David Celeste, whoever you are, fetch help! Can't you see this man is injured?!
16 minutes ago · Like · 👍 4

Tim My heart! God help me in my time of need!
16 minutes ago · Like · 👍 1

Lizzie HA its happening again!
16 minutes ago · Like · 👍 1

Steve fuck u guys!!!!
15 minutes ago · Like · 👍 2

David For heaven's sake, Celeste, pick up the phone and dial 999!
15 minutes ago · Like · 👍 4

Tim What happened? Why am I in such pain?
14 minutes ago · Like · 👍 1

David I'm so sorry – it's the damn kids – night and day they hound me! I just couldn't take it anymore so I set a trap.
14 minutes ago · Like · 👍 4

Tim Are you joking?
13 minutes ago · Like · 👍 1

David No, this isn't a joke. Believe me, there's absolutely nothing funny going on here.
13 minutes ago · Like · 👍 4

Steve u 2 need to get a life!
12 minutes ago · Like · 👍 1

David Call the emergency services right now, woman! THIS IS CELESTE TIME I'M TELLING YOU.
12 minutes ago · Like · 👍 2

Steve u ar all dicks
11 minutes ago · Like · 👍 1

Lizzie bwa ha ha!
11 minutes ago · Like · 👍 1

Tim Chest bumps till the end of time.
10 minutes ago · Like · 👍 7

Apologies

In the last edition of this book I joked that the best remedy for insomnia was a hundred Paracetamol. It's since been brought to my attention that a child could take that remark at face value and act upon it. For that I sincerely apologise.

A child can get a good night's sleep on fifty Paracetamol, sixty tops.

A word from our sponsor

Credits

Choreography by Paula Abdul.

Actual credits to prove I am not a monster

For my wife, Adriana. I like you.

For Dad and Mum (in no particular order).

And for my proof readers:

Alex Musson
James Rose
Joel Soetendorp
Ed O'Meara
Michelle Strutt
Kevin Murphy
Chrissie Dalziel
Lindsay Sharman
Pen Avey
Jeremy Orbell
Stu Richards
Matthew Stott
Nig Lovell
Bryan Romaine *

* Note: In the event of a single overlooked typo, please consider these offers of gratitude unilaterally withdrown.

Also by David Bussell

Bad Endings

Available from Amazon.